Burie

The True Story of Fred and Rose West and the Secrets Beneath 25 Cromwell Street

By

Reeve Kellan

CONTENTS

Preface

When I first began researching the story of Fred and Rose West, I didn't set out to write about horror. What drew me instead was the quiet question behind every tragedy: How does such evil grow where ordinary life once stood?

The Wests' house at 25 Cromwell Street had been just another home on a busy road in Gloucester—ordinary on the outside, unspeakable within. Beneath its floorboards and behind its walls, the evidence of cruelty went unnoticed for years, hidden beneath layers of charm, manipulation, and silence. What fascinated me was not the gruesomeness of their acts but the deception that held a family and a community in its grip.

As I read police statements, court transcripts, and survivor testimonies, I began to see more than a case file. I saw lives stolen from time, voices still echoing from a place where truth had been buried, literally and figuratively. Writing this book became less about retelling crime and more about restoring humanity to those who lost it.

I approach this work not as a voyeur of tragedy but as a witness. Every page was written with restraint, compassion, and the belief that understanding—even the darkest truths—can help prevent them from taking root again.

There are no heroes here, only people: some who failed to see, some who tried to speak, and others who endured. My hope is that, by bringing their stories into light, readers might remember the human cost of neglect, secrecy, and fear.

This book is not about Fred and Rose West's notoriety. It is about the people whose lives they erased—and the courage it took to unearth what was buried beneath 25 Cromwell Street.

Introduction

On a gray February morning in 1994, a small team of detectives and forensic officers gathered in front of a modest terraced house at 25 Cromwell Street, Gloucester. To passersby, it looked like any other home—peeling paint, narrow windows, a small gate leading to the street. But that morning, the house had stopped being ordinary. It had become a crime scene.

The police had come looking for a young woman who had vanished years earlier, but what they found instead was far beyond a missing person case. The search began quietly, with shovels breaking the cold earth beneath the patio. The first bones uncovered were small, almost fragile. Within days, they would uncover more—each discovery unfolding a story of decades-long violence, control, and secrets buried in silence.

Fred West, a builder known for his talkative charm, and his wife, Rose, a woman whose calm demeanor hid something far darker, were about to face the reckoning of their lives. To the outside world, they had seemed an odd but ordinary couple—raising children, taking in lodgers, chatting with neighbors. Behind closed doors, however, a campaign of abuse and murder had stretched back over twenty years.

This book traces that journey: from Fred's troubled childhood in rural Herefordshire to the moment he met Rose, through their years together at Cromwell Street, and the chilling legacy they left behind. It follows the detectives who pieced together the puzzle, the survivors who found their voices, and the community that learned too late what had been happening in its midst.

Every chapter seeks to show not only what happened, but how—and why—ordinary settings can mask extraordinary darkness. The Wests' story is not just about crime. It is about control, deception, and the silent spaces where victims disappear long before their bodies are found.

To understand 25 Cromwell Street is to confront uncomfortable truths about human behavior: how cruelty hides in plain sight, how society often overlooks the vulnerable, and how truth—once unearthed—can finally speak for those who no longer can.

Chapter 1

Shadows Beneath the Hills

Т he hills of Herefordshire have always seemed timeless—rolling fields stitched together by hedgerows and small stone cottages, the kind of landscape that hides more than it reveals. In the years after the Second World War, those hills carried the smell of turned soil and diesel engines, the rhythm of farm work marking the passage of seasons. It was here, in this quiet countryside, that Frederick Walter Stephen West was born in September 1941—a child of earth, isolation, and uneasy silence.

Fred's early world was narrow. His family farm, Moorcourt Cottage, stood on the outskirts of Much Marcle, a small village surrounded by orchards. The farmhouse was drafty and dim, with more animals than people moving through its yard. His father, Walter, was known locally as a hardworking but rough man—quick with his hands, quicker with his temper. His mother, Daisy, was stern and protective, the sort of woman who believed family business stayed behind closed doors.

Neighbors recalled little warmth in the West household. Fred and his five siblings grew up in a home where obedience was expected and affection was rare. Walter taught his sons to work the land, fix machinery, and hunt small game, but he also taught them something darker—the idea that authority gave permission. The boundaries between discipline and cruelty, between right and wrong, were already blurred before Fred could understand what either word meant.

As a boy, he was small, restless, and eager to please. Those who knew him described a nervous energy, a constant need for attention. In school, his teachers found him slow to learn but quick to charm; he would grin his way out of trouble, make jokes when caught lying, and imitate accents to win laughter. Beneath the surface, though, that charm was already an armor.

The rural poverty of postwar Britain shaped him as much as his family did. There were few comforts and fewer choices. For young men in the countryside, options were limited: farming, building, or leaving. But Fred was drawn to movement. He rode motorbikes through narrow lanes, tinkered with engines, and spent long hours in barns where he could be alone. Even then, solitude seemed to soothe him more than company.

Stories circulated later—dark rumors about the West household. Some claimed that Daisy was possessive to the point of obsession, that she blurred maternal care with control. Others spoke of Walter's crude jokes and the way his sons mimicked them. These were the whispers that only surfaced after the truth came out decades later, when people tried to make sense of what could have shaped a man like Fred. At the time, though, no one asked questions. In a place like Much Marcle, people minded their own business.

By his mid-teens, Fred had dropped out of school and begun working on farms. He was wiry, confident, and often in trouble. He chased local girls, boasted about fights, and carried a reputation for arrogance. Yet, beneath the swagger was an insecurity he never seemed to outrun—a sense that he was lesser, unwanted, and constantly at risk of being found out.

In 1958, at the age of seventeen, Fred was involved in his first serious accident. Riding his motorcycle along a country road, he collided with another vehicle and was thrown headfirst onto the pavement. His skull fractured; his nose was crushed. He spent a week in a coma and emerged changed—his memory unreliable, his temper shorter. Those close to him said he became unpredictable after that, alternating between charm and sudden rage, as if the injury had loosened something that had once been held together by will.

After the accident, Fred's behavior grew stranger. He began stealing, lying without cause, and showing no fear of consequence. He seemed almost amused by danger, treating every warning as a challenge. Some psychiatrists would later argue that the head trauma deepened traits already present in him—impulsivity, detachment, and a lack of empathy. Whatever the cause, the young man who walked away from that crash was not the same one who had ridden into it.

A few years later, he met a girl named Catherine Costello—known to friends as Rena. She was Scottish, vivacious, and searching for something better than what life had offered her so far. Fred met her while working as a laborer in Ledbury, and he was quick to flatter her with jokes and small gifts. To Rena, he seemed adventurous—a man who could build, fix, and promise a kind of life that felt exciting after years of hardship.

They married in 1962, when Fred was twenty-one and Rena was pregnant. The ceremony was small, the future uncertain. Within months, Fred was already restless again. He drifted between jobs, often vanishing for days, sometimes returning with stories of work that never existed. His need for control began to show early in the marriage—jealousy, suspicion, and the expectation that

Rena would obey. When she didn't, his anger turned physical.

By 1964, the couple had moved to Scotland, living in cramped flats and surviving on low wages. Rena gave birth to two daughters—Charmaine and Anne Marie—but domestic life did nothing to settle Fred. He was drawn to petty theft, to secret affairs, and to the growing thrill of power over others. The cycle of violence that would later define his life had already begun, though no one outside the marriage yet saw its depth.

One night, after an argument that spilled into the street, Fred was arrested for theft and sexual assault. He spent several months in jail, and by the time he was released, Rena had left him. She tried to start anew, but Fred followed her south, tracking her movements with unsettling persistence. His need to control her—and the children—was rooted less in love than in ownership. He couldn't stand to be ignored.

In 1967, Rena briefly took him back, perhaps out of fear, perhaps hope. That same year, Fred met a woman named Rosemary Letts. She was fifteen, working as a bread shop assistant in Cheltenham, and drawn to Fred's confidence. Their meeting would mark the moment when two unstable lives began to intertwine, feeding each other's darkness.

But before that convergence—before Cromwell Street, before the concrete and the hidden graves—there was this boy from the hills. A boy who had learned early that silence could hide anything. The countryside that raised him was quiet, unchanging, forgiving. It did not question what happened behind doors, and in that silence, Fred West learned how to become invisible.

As years went on, he carried those lessons with him—the ability to smile through deceit, to charm without empathy, to hurt without remorse. The fields he once walked as a boy became distant memories, replaced by city streets where his cruelty would grow unchecked. Yet, somewhere in the background of every future crime lay the echo of those early shadows: the hills, the farmhouse, the boy who had never truly been taught what humanity meant.

The origins of Fred West's violence did not lie in one single event. They were the slow accumulation of neglect, control, and unchecked impulses—small cruelties that hardened over time. He was both a product of his environment and the architect of his own ruin.

When investigators decades later sifted through his history, they found no single explanation that could justify what came next. What they did find, buried within old police files and school reports, was a boy who had learned that attention—whether from kindness or fear—was better than being unseen. That belief would define his life, and it would destroy countless others.

By the time Fred West left the hills of Herefordshire behind, he was already carrying everything he needed to become what he would later be known for: a man who built walls to hide his crimes, who smiled while he lied, and who mistook domination for love.

The quiet countryside faded into memory, but its silence—its tolerance of what should have been confronted—would follow him all the way to Gloucester. And there, on a narrow street lined with identical houses, the shadows beneath the hills would find their darkest echo.

Chapter 2

The Making of a Predator

L eaving the quiet folds of Herefordshire behind, Fred West carried with him more than the smell of soil and diesel that clung to his clothes. He carried a private code—one learned in isolation, in a family that measured worth through dominance and obedience. When he stepped into early adulthood, that code became his compass. The world outside the farm was wider, faster, and, for Fred, filled with opportunities to test just how far his charm and defiance could take him.

Drifting Years

The early 1960s found him moving from one labouring job to another—construction sites in Gloucester, fruit-picking farms in Ledbury, road crews that travelled wherever the work was. He was known as a capable builder with strong hands and a knack for repair, but he was unreliable. Pay packets vanished in pubs; foremen replaced him without fuss. Each dismissal only strengthened his belief that rules applied to everyone but him.

He lived mostly in rented rooms or cheap lodgings, rooms that smelled of paint thinner and damp, where he could disappear between jobs without anyone asking questions. To strangers, Fred was talkative, sometimes even funny. He could disarm suspicion with a grin, and when that failed, he turned sullen in an instant. People remembered his eyes—restless, quick to narrow whenever he felt challenged.

That volatility often flared in small acts first: petty theft, threats, the reckless use of his motorbike as a weapon of pride. Local police knew his name long before they knew his crimes. Reports from that decade record minor offences, nothing that hinted at what he would later become. Yet, each incident added a layer of confidence that punishment would always miss him.

The Accident's Shadow

The head injury from 1958 never truly healed. Doctors noted the skull fracture, but not the invisible damage beneath it—the shifts in temperament, the memory gaps, the sudden rages. He told friends that his "head went funny sometimes." Those who worked with him learned to avoid eye contact when that change came over him. One moment he could be telling a crude joke; the next, his tone dropped cold, as though he had stepped outside himself.

In later assessments, psychologists described this blend of impulsivity and callousness as the seed of his predatory behavior. He had lost whatever internal gate once slowed his urges. Violence felt natural, consequence abstract.

Rena and the Spiral

It was during this unsettled period that he met Catherine "Rena" Costello, a young woman from Glasgow who had drifted south in search of work. She was spirited, fond of laughter, and used to surviving on charm as well. To her, Fred's accent and bravado made him seem worldly. He promised safety and adventure, and within months they married.

Domestic life, however, did not soften him. When Rena's independence clashed with his need for control, arguments became routine. He accused her of betrayal, demanded to know where she went, whom she spoke to. Neighbors heard shouting through the thin walls of their small flats, the noise fading as quickly as it began. Rena often re-appeared with forced smiles and long sleeves even in warm weather.

The relationship lurched between affection and terror. Fred's jealousy was obsessive; he watched her every movement yet spent nights away, claiming work in distant towns. Rena's attempts to leave were brief; he always found her. Friends later said she seemed trapped between fear and pity, convinced he might change if only life steadied.

Work and Wandering

By 1964 Fred was back in England, taking construction work wherever he could find it. He lived cheaply, slept in caravans, and grew fascinated by the freedom of the road. The anonymity suited him. He could start fresh in every town, inventing small histories that made him sound successful.

He began driving for hire, offering rides to hitchhikers and young women commuting between nearby towns. Most of these encounters passed without incident, but each gave him a sense of control—someone dependent on his goodwill, even for a short time. That feeling of command became addictive.

Police records from the mid-1960s mention complaints about a man matching Fred's description harassing women near bus stops and cafés. None of the reports led to charges; the victims either withdrew or could not identify him positively. Fred learned from those escapes. He refined how he approached, how he hid impatience behind jokes, how he gauged fear.

The Fractures Deepen

Family connections eroded. Fred's parents had long since despaired of his behavior, though Daisy still defended him fiercely. When he returned home, she fed him, praised him, and told others he was "misunderstood." That blind devotion reinforced his belief that he was special, chosen somehow to live outside the rules that bound ordinary men.

By 1966, Rena's patience had collapsed. She fled to Scotland with their two small daughters. Fred followed, alternating threats and apologies until she reluctantly allowed him back. Those around them noticed the strain—his possessiveness, her exhaustion. In letters discovered years later, Rena confided to a friend that she feared "he'll hurt someone one day."

That prediction proved tragically prescient. When Rena disappeared soon after, few people noticed. She had moved often, rarely wrote home, and Fred offered a casual explanation: she'd gone abroad. Her friend Ann McFall, a quiet young woman who had once helped look after the children, also vanished. For decades, their names would linger only in missing-person files.

Isolation and Control

After those disappearances, Fred's behavior changed subtly. He spoke less about family and more about work. He moved to the West Midlands, living near Cheltenham, where he found steady employment as a builder. Outwardly, he seemed to be improving—steady job, small social circle, few visible troubles. Inside, the same compulsions simmered, disciplined now by caution. He had learned how to conceal himself.

Colleagues noticed that he avoided drinking heavily in public; he preferred to keep his wits. He laughed about past arrests as if they were pranks, proof of his cleverness. When confronted, he could look directly into a person's eyes without blinking, his voice calm, his expression unreadable.

Neighbors described him as friendly but intrusive. He offered to fix things—fences, steps, wiring—and often did so uninvited. He liked being owed gratitude. Every small act of help established a thread of power.

The Pattern Takes Shape

Looking back, investigators would identify this period as the creation of Fred West's pattern. His life became a cycle of work, control, and secret indulgence. He built trust only to exploit it, studied people's weaknesses the way a builder studied blueprints. Each successful deception convinced him that no one would ever expose him.

He also discovered the practical skills that would later serve darker purposes: how to mix concrete, how to reinforce walls, how to repair floors without leaving a trace. These trades gave him not only a living but the means to conceal one.

Psychologists reviewing his later confessions saw in these years a transition from impulsive aggression to premeditated cruelty. The physical labor, the isolation, the small acts of dominance—all trained him for the life he was constructing. He was learning to engineer secrecy.

Cheltenham and the Watcher

By 1967 Fred was spending evenings in Cheltenham cafés, watching people more than speaking. He favored tables near windows, where he could observe the movement of passers-by. He noticed patterns—who walked alone, who seemed shy, who hesitated before crossing the road. Observation became another tool, a silent rehearsal for control.

It was in one of these cafés that he first saw a teenage girl named Rosemary Letts. She was serving behind the counter, quick-smiling, slightly awkward, still half-child. To Fred, she was an opportunity wrapped in innocence. To Rose, he was attention from an older man who seemed confident and kind. The moment passed unnoticed by everyone else, but it marked the joining of two unstable lives.

The Psychology of Power

Fred's shift from impulsive offender to calculated predator was not sudden. It unfolded through small decisions: the choice to pursue instead of release, to lie instead of admit, to conceal instead of confront. Each decision dulled empathy further.

Those who later studied his behavior described him as possessing a working cruelty—violence used as a tool rather than an explosion. He tested limits constantly, not from passion but curiosity. Could he frighten without consequence? Could he take without being stopped? The success of each experiment became proof of his invincibility.

The years between 1964 and 1967 were therefore his apprenticeship in domination. He learned to read fear as clearly as language and to manipulate affection until it became dependence. In that mastery he found purpose.

The Road Ahead

By the time Fred West met Rosemary Letts, he was thirty-six, though his weathered face made him look older. He owned little more than his tools and his vehicle, but he carried an unwavering belief that he could shape people as easily as he shaped plaster. Rose, fifteen and eager to escape a troubled home, saw in him the freedom she lacked.

Their connection would fuse Fred's learned cruelty with Rose's emerging instability, transforming solitary predation into partnership. But that story—the slow construction of the house at Cromwell Street, the silence it would hold—belonged to the years ahead.

For now, in the late 1960s, Fred West stood at the threshold of his final evolution. The countryside boy who once hid behind charm had become a man who no longer needed disguise. His world was a blueprint of control, each person around him a structure to be built, used, and dismantled.

When investigators later charted his life, they found no mystery in how he became what he was. The evidence was written in every forgotten warning, every ignored complaint, every silence that allowed him to keep moving. The making of a predator is rarely sudden. It is patient, practiced, and often invisible—until the damage can no longer be buried.

Chapter 3

A Meeting Written in Darkness

The year was 1967. The air in Cheltenham carried the smell of rain and petrol, the scent of a small English town caught between the quiet of tradition and the stirrings of change. In cafés along the high street, teenagers with beehive haircuts gathered after school, their laughter rising above the hiss of coffee machines. Somewhere among them was a girl who would soon become one half of one of Britain's most notorious partnerships. Her name was Rosemary Letts.

Fred West, then in his mid-thirties, was living on the edge of respectability. To anyone passing him on the street, he looked like an ordinary tradesman—rough hands, patched jacket, a man who worked hard and lived simply. Behind that everyday face, however, was a man who had already crossed invisible lines. He had learned how to charm, how to hide, and how to turn vulnerability into opportunity. The quiet streets of Cheltenham suited him. They offered anonymity, and in anonymity, he found freedom.

He first saw her one gray afternoon in a small café off the main road. She was serving at the counter, a slim figure with brown hair that framed a shy but alert face. Her eyes lifted briefly as he ordered tea. She smiled the way people do when politeness is second nature. That fleeting moment—unnoticed by everyone else—marked the beginning of a relationship that would alter countless lives.

Rosemary, called Rose by family and friends, had grown up in a house ruled by tension. Born in Devon in 1953, she had moved frequently as a child. Her father, a man known for strict control and volatile moods, overshadowed the household. Her mother's fragile health added to the instability. The family's frequent relocations left Rose isolated, her schooling interrupted, her friendships brief. By the time she reached her mid-teens, she was hungry for affection—any affection that felt stable and kind.

Fred West noticed that need immediately. He had an instinct for weakness, a practiced eye that recognized loneliness as clearly as others recognized beauty. To Rose, he appeared worldly, confident, and independent—a man who seemed to have control over his life, something she had never known. Their first conversations were simple, almost clumsy: talk of work, family, the weather. He made her laugh. She made him feel admired.

At first, their meetings were accidental—at least that's how Fred made them appear. He would park his van near the café, timing his visits for when she finished her shifts. Soon, he began offering her rides home. The gesture seemed kind, protective even. Rose accepted. Each journey lengthened by a few minutes, each conversation peeling away her hesitation.

People who knew Rose at the time would later describe her as naïve but eager to please, a girl who didn't yet understand the weight of trust. To her family, Fred was a concern. He was twice her age, already married, with children he rarely mentioned. But to Rose, those were details drowned out by his attention. He listened. He flattered. He made her believe that life with him would be freer than the one she knew.

Within months, their relationship deepened. Fred presented himself as a man wronged by circumstance— abandoned, misunderstood, trying to rebuild his life. Rose, full of sympathy, believed she could help him. It was a pattern that had repeated itself with others before her: his ability to reshape the truth into something pitiable. He needed control; she needed purpose. Together, they filled each other's voids.

Those who saw them together spoke of an odd balance between them. Fred seemed proud, almost possessive, while Rose followed his lead with quiet loyalty. Neighbors noticed the way she looked to him before speaking, the way he monitored her movements with casual authority. Yet to outsiders, they still appeared as an unlikely but affectionate couple—a man grateful for a young woman's devotion, a girl transformed by attention she had never received.

By 1969, Rose had moved in with Fred. Her parents' protests were loud but futile. Her father, particularly, forbade the relationship, warning her that Fred was dangerous. But rebellion had taken root in Rose, the kind of rebellion that comes not from strength but from exhaustion. She was tired of being told what to fear. Living with Fred felt like a choice—her choice—and that illusion of freedom was powerful.

Inside the modest homes they occupied, daily life seemed ordinary at first. Fred worked long hours on construction jobs, coming home with dirt on his clothes and stories of work that rarely added up. Rose kept the rooms tidy, cooked meals, and cared for the children Fred brought with him. There were moments of laughter, of routine, even of calm. But underneath that calm ran an undercurrent of control. Fred's rules were subtle at first, presented as suggestions—when to shop, how to dress, whom to avoid. Slowly, those suggestions hardened into orders.

Rose adapted. Whether through fear, loyalty, or the strange comfort of submission, she accepted the structure he imposed. She began to echo his moods, his phrases, even his justifications. In many ways, Fred had found not just a partner but a reflection—a person who would reinforce his worldview rather than challenge it.

For Rose, the transformation was gradual, almost invisible to herself. The girl who had once flinched at her father's voice now learned to quiet her own doubts. She followed Fred's lead in everything, believing that obedience meant safety. Yet beneath that surface obedience, something else was forming—a growing hardness, a numbness that made cruelty seem ordinary.

The years between 1968 and 1970 cemented their bond. They moved between Gloucester and Cheltenham, taking small rented houses and caravans. Fred introduced Rose to his children from previous relationships, weaving new layers of responsibility around her. Each step pulled her deeper into his world, a world built on secrecy and control.

By the time they settled permanently in Gloucester, the foundation of their partnership was complete. What had begun as a meeting of two wounded souls had evolved into something far darker—a shared identity shaped by dominance and dependency. They were no longer separate people but a single, destructive force, each validating the other's impulses.

When police later retraced their steps, witnesses spoke of how inseparable they seemed, how Rose's laughter often followed Fred's jokes even when no one else found them funny. Friends who once pitied her began to avoid them both. The atmosphere around the couple grew heavy, uneasy. There was something about their closeness that felt wrong, though few could have guessed the depth of what lay beneath it.

In hindsight, the story of their meeting reads almost inevitable. Two damaged individuals drawn together by need—his for control, hers for belonging. The darkness that would later define them did not erupt in an instant; it crept forward quietly, concealed beneath gestures of love and normalcy.

When Fred looked at Rose, he saw someone he could shape. When Rose looked at Fred, she saw someone who made her feel significant. It was a meeting written in darkness, and from that moment on, the shadows around them would only grow thicker.

Chapter 4

The House at Cromwell Street

The house at 25 Cromwell Street stood quietly in the heart of Gloucester, unremarkable at first glance—one among many narrow, aging terraces that lined the street. Its brickwork was soot-stained, its windows slightly fogged from years of condensation, and its front garden was more of an afterthought than a space. Yet, behind its faded façade, the house would become the darkest address in Britain, the setting where cruelty was not only concealed but carefully arranged.

When Fred and Rosemary West first moved into the property in 1972, it was little more than a cramped shell. They took a mortgage through a small local firm, pooling together their savings and small earnings from Fred's building work. The early days inside Cromwell Street had a strange sense of purpose—Fred was a man who loved to build, tear down, and build again. He immediately began working on the basement, extending it, reinforcing the walls, and creating what he called "storage spaces." Neighbors often saw him covered in dust and concrete, his face glowing with satisfaction. What no one could see, however, was the slow creation of a hidden world beneath their feet.

The couple's children played in the front yard while Fred worked. Rosemary, then in her early twenties, had taken on the role of both mother and partner in crime, though few understood the extent of her involvement. Inside the house, she ran things with cold efficiency. She kept lodgers—young women, students, or drifters looking for a cheap room. The Wests offered just that, along with a façade of domestic normality. Rent was low, meals were shared occasionally, and Fred would joke with tenants as if he were their friend. To outsiders, it looked like a working-class family doing its best to get by.

But soon, that ordinary image began to warp. The house took on a strange atmosphere that unsettled anyone who stayed too long. Some lodgers complained of hearing muffled noises at night—whispers, crying, or the rhythmic thud of footsteps descending into the basement after midnight. Others spoke of Rosemary's sudden bursts of temper, her icy glare when someone overstayed a conversation, her quickness to end friendships without reason. Within those walls, control and submission became a daily ritual.

Fred's modifications to the property grew increasingly complex. He added soundproofing to the cellar, explaining to neighbors that it was for "band practice" or "motor work." He built hidden compartments behind the walls, hollow spaces beneath the floorboards, and a deep pit under the basement that he lined with concrete. No one questioned his renovations too closely; after all, he was a builder by trade. But the purpose was far from innocent.

It was in this basement that the first of several victims would disappear forever. The air down there was damp, the single light bulb weak, and the smell of earth never quite faded. Fred called it his "special room." It was where he believed he had full control—no interruptions, no judgment, just the terrifying freedom to act out the darkness that had taken root in him years earlier. Rosemary's involvement deepened. She didn't merely tolerate his violence; she participated, feeding on the control it gave her. Together, they created a partnership of domination that blurred the line between desire and destruction.

Upstairs, life continued as usual. Their children learned not to ask questions. They were taught obedience, silence, and fear. The sound of the basement door opening after dark became something no one dared mention. The Wests' façade remained intact. Rosemary went shopping in the city, her hair neatly styled, chatting with store owners about her growing family. Fred was friendly with neighbors, offering help with small repairs. He smiled often, laughed easily, and hid the rot beneath the charm.

By the late 1970s, 25 Cromwell Street had taken on a rhythm of horror disguised as domestic life. Visitors came and went. Lodgers were welcomed and then vanished. When neighbors asked, Fred always had explanations— one had moved abroad, another had gone home suddenly, another had left with a boyfriend. His stories were delivered so confidently that people believed him. After all, the Wests seemed settled, respectable enough. Who could imagine that beneath their feet, a room of death had been carved into the earth itself?

Fred's obsession with secrecy became almost artistic. He boasted to Rosemary about how clever he was, how no one would ever find out. "They don't look too close," he once told her. "People see what they want to see." That philosophy guided everything he did—hide in plain sight, and the world will never think to look beneath.

As the years passed, the house began to feel cursed even to those who knew nothing of its true nature. Tenants often left without warning. Friends who visited once rarely came again. The laughter of children echoed strangely against the walls, as though the building itself absorbed sorrow. The smell of freshly poured concrete lingered too often, and the basement door was always locked.

Fred's construction work eventually slowed, but his projects at home never stopped. There was always another wall to reinforce, another patch of flooring to conceal. Rosemary, meanwhile, tightened her grip on the household, ruling with an iron will. To disobey her, even slightly, meant punishment. She was no longer merely assisting Fred—she was shaping him, matching his cruelty, sometimes surpassing it. Together, they created a home that was both fortress and prison, sanctuary and tomb.

By the time the 1980s arrived, 25 Cromwell Street was infamous among those who had briefly crossed its threshold. Few could explain why, but everyone seemed to sense something wrong. Children from neighboring homes crossed the street to avoid its shadow. Delivery men hurried their work. The Wests, however, appeared content in their small empire of secrecy.

In a twisted way, the house reflected its owners perfectly—ordinary on the outside, unspeakable within. Every brick seemed to hold a memory, every room a whisper. And beneath it all, in the concrete silence of the cellar, the truth was waiting—patient, buried, and unholy.

The house would stand for decades, weathering rain and rumor, until the day investigators would finally break through its layers and uncover what lay beneath. But for now, in those early years, it thrived as the perfect disguise—a quiet home on an ordinary street, hiding the work of monsters who believed they were invisible.

Chapter 5

Children of

Silence

B y the early 1970s, 25 Cromwell Street had settled into its rhythm, a home outwardly ordinary yet quietly threaded with control and fear. Within its narrow walls, the West children grew up not knowing what normal meant. The oldest, Heather, Fred's daughter from his first marriage, already carried the burden of awareness; she witnessed the subtle tyrannies Fred imposed on those around him and felt the tension of his unpredictability in ways a child could never fully name. Soon, the household would swell with more children—by the mid-1970s, Fred and Rosemary were raising a large family together. There were biological children, stepchildren, and lodgers, but in the West home, the distinctions mattered little. Each child existed first and foremost under the dominion of their parents, particularly Fred, whose gaze could pierce even the most innocent moment.

Everyday life was a lesson in vigilance. The children learned quickly that disobedience, no matter how minor, could trigger immediate punishment. Silence became a shield, compliance a survival tactic. There were rules spoken and unspoken: never question Fred, never contradict Rosemary, never linger too long in any room alone. The Wests' household was structured almost militarily, with invisible boundaries that were as much psychological as physical. The children adapted—small gestures of compliance became habits; tiny acts of defiance were calculated, hidden, or abandoned altogether.

Heather and her siblings witnessed and endured patterns that were methodical and relentless. Chores were never casual; they were tests of obedience. Meals, though routine, were often overshadowed by tension: the wrong expression, the wrong tone, could elicit sharp reprimands or cruel laughter. Fred's mood was unpredictable; a calm morning could shift in an instant to a storm of rage, while Rosemary, whose temperament was equally formidable, reinforced compliance with cold efficiency. The children learned the language of fear almost as naturally as the language of love, though the two were forever entwined.

As more children came into the household, the circle of control widened. Newborns and toddlers were not merely cared for; they were indoctrinated into the same silent understanding, their innocence overshadowed by the weight of adult power. The West children did not know freedom as other children did—they knew structure, hierarchy, and the omnipresent threat of reprisal. Playing outside was limited and monitored; friendships beyond the household were fleeting. The street, the schoolyard, and even neighbors' homes were distant worlds, glimpsed through careful, watchful eyes.

Lodgers arrived periodically, often young women seeking a room or a fresh start, unaware of the dangers lurking behind the façade of the Wests' normality. To the children, the lodgers were both companions and warnings. They observed the adults' interactions, the subtle tests of obedience, the coercive tactics that began with charm and ended in terror. Some lodgers departed quickly, leaving behind stories whispered by the children in secret. Others vanished without explanation, their absence stitched into the children's consciousness as an unspoken truth: the house consumed those who stayed too long.

The basement, once merely a workshop, became a space of terror and fascination. To the children, it was forbidden territory, a place where sounds came from deep shadows and where adults' authority was absolute. Fred's insistence that no one enter without permission was backed by implicit and explicit threats. Rosemary's oversight was no gentler. Through this, the children internalized obedience not as a choice but as necessity. Even play was constrained by unspoken rules, laughter dampened by the awareness of listening ears.

Education outside the home offered little relief. Teachers noted quiet, compliant children, quick to please but slow to speak of anything personal. School was a place of routine, but the emotional scars of Cromwell Street followed them quietly: hesitation, self-monitoring, and a constant anticipation of anger. The children adapted with astonishing resilience, masking the fear with smiles and polite gestures, all while absorbing the unspeakable lessons of dominance and control.

As the 1970s progressed, the cycle of cruelty at Cromwell Street became increasingly entrenched. The children grew older, some beginning to sense that the household was different, dangerous even, though comprehension lagged behind instinct. Heather, in particular, bore witness to the darker aspects of the Wests' pattern—the disappearances, the whispered threats, the chilling casualness with which Fred and Rosemary exerted power over others. For the youngest children, life was confusion, obedience, and survival, their world a series of rooms, staircases, and locked doors, punctuated by the adult presence that governed every detail.

The house itself became a character in their childhood: walls that hid secrets, floors that bore weight in silence, and ceilings that trapped sound. The concrete and wood were more than construction; they were instruments of control. Every renovation Fred undertook, every compartment hidden, reinforced the house's dual identity as home and prison. The children learned to navigate it carefully, aware that any misstep could trigger punishment or worse.

By the end of the decade, Cromwell Street had solidified into a landscape of dominance, secrecy, and terror. The children, molded by fear and routine, were silent observers, witnesses to acts they could neither fully comprehend nor report. Their lives were intertwined with the rhythms of cruelty, and survival depended on invisibility, obedience, and quiet compliance. Yet even within that suffocating environment, the children exhibited resilience: small gestures of defiance, whispered secrets between siblings, and moments of fleeting joy that could not be entirely extinguished.

In retrospect, investigators would later recognize that these formative years at Cromwell Street shaped not only the children's survival strategies but also their understanding of morality, trust, and danger. Silence, once a shield, became a habit. Fear, once a response, became a constant companion. The West children lived in a house that was both home and nightmare, learning that the line between the two was determined entirely by the whims of their parents.

By the time law enforcement would finally intervene decades later, the children's world had been defined by shadow, secrecy, and fear. They were witnesses and victims, their memories a ledger of quiet suffering. Cromwell Street had claimed their innocence, and in its walls, the echoes of their silence would remain long after the adults who ruled it were gone.

Chapter 6

The Vanished and the Forgotten

25 Cromwell Street appeared ordinary to anyone walking past: a modest working-class home in Gloucester, with freshly painted bricks, a neatly trimmed lawn, and curtains drawn in the evenings. Children's laughter occasionally drifted to the street, the clink of cutlery hinted at domestic life, and the faint aroma of cooking or cleaning suggested normality. Yet beneath this ordinary exterior, the house held a darkness so complete that no casual observer could imagine it. Within its walls, fear and control dictated a rhythm invisible to neighbors, a rhythm that had begun long before anyone took note of the subtle irregularities that would later reveal themselves as signs of something profoundly wrong.

For those inside—the children of Fred and Rosemary West—the ordinary and the unimaginable coexisted under one roof. While they continued to perform daily routines, they were learning a delicate balance: silence was safety, observation was survival, and any misstep could carry consequences too severe to name. The house itself was both classroom and prison, shaping their perception of the world from the earliest age.

Fred West maintained a façade of geniality for the outside world. His hands were perpetually coated in concrete dust; his clothes bore traces of mortar, evidence of work done and diligence performed. To neighbors and passersby, he was the affable, helpful tradesman, quick with a smile, a joke, or a friendly greeting. Rosemary's exterior mirrored this normality: bustling efficiently from room to room, she ensured that the children were clean, polite, and obedient, and that the household ran like clockwork. Yet inside, their domestic perfection concealed a carefully orchestrated system of predation, with Fred as the architect and Rosemary as both facilitator and enforcer.

The women who entered Cromwell Street were rarely complete strangers. They were often young, isolated, or vulnerable—lodgers seeking a room, acquaintances seeking guidance, or casual contacts trusting the couple enough to accept help. Fred's charm and apparent generosity lured them in, masking the danger that awaited. Once inside, these women became part of a larger, almost imperceptible pattern: disappearances woven into the very fabric of the house, hidden beneath the rhythm of seemingly ordinary life.

The disappearances were deliberate and precise. Complaints of missing women appeared sporadically in police records, often months after the fact, and were frequently dismissed as voluntary absences. In a small city like Gloucester, these anomalies blended into the ordinary flow of life. Social norms discouraged scrutiny of working-class households, while the limited resources of the local police left gaps in investigative capacity. Even neighbors who glimpsed fleeting irregularities—lodgers arriving and leaving abruptly, young women who stayed only briefly, occasional muffled screams—rarely acted. Suspicion never fully crystallized; the house's façade of normalcy remained convincing.

Fred's methodology was meticulous. He observed potential victims for isolation, lack of family oversight, and vulnerability. His friendly demeanor and helpfulness were carefully measured, intended to build trust without arousing suspicion. Rosemary's role evolved alongside him. Initially compliant, she soon became an active participant, reinforcing Fred's authority and subtly manipulating the women who came to the house. Together, they established a dual system of domination: Fred enforced physical and psychological control, while Rosemary provided emotional manipulation and validation, creating dependency. The victims' autonomy eroded gradually, ensnared in routines where fear was omnipresent yet nearly invisible to outsiders.

Among the early victims were women who would later appear in official missing-person files, quietly absorbed into Gloucester's collective memory. For the West children, each vanishing was an unspoken lesson. Observing these disappearances, they understood—though not fully—the danger of attention and curiosity. Questions were dangerous, observation was necessary, and silence was survival. The children internalized rules they did not yet understand, their consciousness quietly shaping itself around the household's secrets.

Fred's skills as a builder allowed him to transform Cromwell Street into a house of concealment. Hidden compartments, reinforced floors, false walls, and a labyrinthine basement became both repositories and prisons. Wood, concrete, and craftsmanship were turned into instruments of erasure. Victims were not merely absent; they were folded into the structure itself, hidden in plain sight. Rosemary ensured appearances were maintained, preparing plausible explanations for any who inquired: a girl had moved abroad, another returned to relatives, another left for work. The house projected normalcy so convincingly that those outside were rarely suspicious.

The Wests' control extended beyond concealment to psychological manipulation. The women in the house were gradually stripped of autonomy, drawn into routines where compliance was rewarded and hesitation punished. Obedience was reinforced subtly, through small gestures, words, and threats—both implied and explicit. Those who stayed too long risked disappearance. Those who questioned the household's rules were subtly coerced or silenced. Those who observed too much—such as lodgers aware of more than they should—faced consequences designed to erase their existence.

The 1970s moved into the 1980s, and the pattern of disappearances intensified. Only in hindsight, after painstaking reconstruction of police files, witness statements, and fragmentary accounts, did the scale of the Wests' crimes become clear. Patterns that had been invisible to casual observers revealed themselves: lodgers who never returned, young women whose presence was suddenly erased, hushed conversations about departures that seemed to happen without notice. The children began to notice too, piecing together fragments of these absences. Yet instinctive fear prevented intervention, leaving comprehension behind awareness. Silence remained the only path to safety.

Psychologists later described the household as an environment of learned helplessness for the children, and a laboratory of calculated predation for the victims. Each disappearance reinforced the Wests' sense of control; each concealment honed their methods of domination. The house operated as a classroom, teaching obedience, fear, and compliance by observation and enforced through threat. The children were unwilling students, and the victims unwilling participants in the unspoken curriculum of Cromwell Street.

The ordinary rhythms of life persisted alongside the horrific pattern. Children attended school, played with friends under careful supervision, and interacted with neighbors. But every gesture, every casual laugh, every chore was underscored by invisible rules: who held power, who could vanish, and who was temporarily safe. Even routine acts were colored by awareness, creating a tension that threaded daily life with invisible danger.

Over the years, a grim timeline of disappearances unfolded, stretching back decades. Only decades later, during meticulous investigations, did the breadth of the Wests' crimes become apparent. Cromwell Street became both a repository for the erased and a stage for the invisible. The children, older and more aware, understood that survival depended on observation, silence, and compliance. They carried the weight of memory—patterns too complex to articulate, faces too vivid to forget.

Through it all, the victims' absence left marks not only on Gloucester but on those who bore witness. Every vanished face, every unspoken story, every unanswered question contributed to a pervasive unease that lingered long after the disappearances. The house itself became defined by the missing: a structure where horror and domestic life coexisted seamlessly, where silence was armor, and secrecy was survival.

By the late 1980s, the duality of Cromwell Street was complete. Each disappearance expanded the Wests' dominion, reinforcing lessons of secrecy, concealment, and orchestration of normalcy. In this house, the vanished were never truly gone; they were folded into walls, floors, and memory, inscribed upon the consciousness of the children who had no choice but to watch, listen, and adapt. Survival demanded compliance. Observation demanded silence. Life and horror existed side by side—inseparable, relentless, and chillingly ordinary.

Chapter 7

Secrets Under the Floorboards

B y the late 1980s, Cromwell Street had become a house of dual realities: to the outside world, it remained a tidy, unremarkable family home; within, it was a stage for horrors meticulously hidden from view. Among the ordinary routines of domestic life—the laughter of children, the clang of dishes, the hum of mundane conversation—lay secrets buried so deeply that even years of neighborhood familiarity could not have uncovered them. And yet, in the quietest corners, beneath the floors, behind false walls, and in the shadows of a basement long feared, those secrets were waiting.

Fred West had always been methodical. As a builder, he had a mind for structure, for hidden spaces, for the ways in which walls, floors, and ceilings could conceal more than dust and old furniture. By the time the house had been extensively renovated, it had become almost a labyrinth, each alteration a calculated measure designed to obscure evidence of the unthinkable. False floorboards in the kitchen, panels in the living room, hidden compartments beneath the stairs—all were part of an intricate system of concealment, an architecture of control and erasure. To Fred, the floorboards were not just timber; they were vaults, repositories for his victims, and extensions of his authority.

Rosemary, equally cunning, understood the power these hidden spaces conferred. While Fred handled the construction, she orchestrated the psychological control of those who came to the house. Every lodger, every acquaintance, every young woman who crossed the threshold was assessed for vulnerability and potential. Once identified, they were slowly drawn into the household, lulled by apparent kindness or help, unaware that beneath the very boards they walked on, a grim certainty awaited.

The house seemed ordinary enough to those who spent only fleeting moments there. To the children, however, every floorboard was a potential sign, every creak a message. They learned to move carefully, to gauge the tone of conversation, and to observe patterns that others would have dismissed. The basement, already a place of fear and fascination, now held additional significance: not only was it a space forbidden and intimidating, it was the locus of the household's most carefully hidden atrocities. Children could sense its power; they knew, in instinctive understanding, that beneath their feet lay truths that were dangerous to name.

It began subtly. Fred would spend hours in quiet, repetitive labor, moving and reinforcing floorboards, installing locks, building cavities into the very structure of the home. To the casual eye, it appeared as ordinary maintenance—repairs, renovations, or enhancements—but for anyone who looked closely, there were signs: slight misalignments in the boards, subtle discoloration of wood, tiny gaps that hinted at something concealed beneath. Rosemary often accompanied him, not with tools but with conversation, keeping the children occupied, ensuring they were occupied, and maintaining the impression that nothing unusual was occurring.

Victims, by contrast, were unaware entirely. They walked the floors, cleaned the rooms, and engaged in the routines Fred and Rosemary had set, oblivious to the danger just beneath their feet. A false sense of safety was critical; it allowed the Wests to operate with precision, to manipulate trust, and to orchestrate disappearances that were both sudden and systematic. Fred's hands, skilled with both mortar and timber, were capable of more than construction—they were instruments of concealment, of the physical erasure of lives from the visible world.

The methods were chilling in their calculated simplicity. A floorboard lifted, a cavity prepared, a victim unobserved—each act followed a rhythm that had been rehearsed and refined over years. For Rosemary, complicity was psychological as much as practical. She ensured that the domestic façade remained flawless, that explanations were ready for any questioning neighbor or visitor, and that the rhythm of normality continued uninterrupted. In the world above the floorboards, domestic life went on—children attended school, chores were performed, neighbors exchanged greetings—while below, the hidden horrors expanded in silence.

It was not only the victims who were affected by the hidden spaces. The children of the house, growing older, increasingly became witnesses to the subtle signals of danger. They noted which rooms were off-limits, which floorboards were treated with extraordinary care, and the patterns of arrivals and sudden disappearances of lodgers. Heather, particularly observant and already attuned to the household's rhythms, began to connect small details into a larger, terrifying pattern. Yet even she, perceptive as she was, could only glimpse fragments; the true scale of what lay under the floorboards was beyond comprehension.

Neighbors occasionally noticed oddities. A faint smell, an unusual sound, a lodger who vanished without explanation. But the Wests' outward normality was convincing. Fred's cheerful assistance, his willingness to help with repairs on other houses, and his ever-present smile were shields. Rosemary's attentiveness and charm created layers of plausibility. What outsiders could not see—and what many never imagined—was that the house itself was complicit in the crimes. Every floorboard, every nail, every hidden cavity was a silent accomplice, keeping the secrets Fred and Rosemary required to maintain control.

By the 1980s, the architecture of concealment had evolved into a complex system that mirrored the psychological manipulation within the household. Victims were trapped not only by physical spaces but by trust and dependency. They were drawn deeper into the home, into the patterns of obedience and compliance that Fred and Rosemary had perfected. And the children continued their silent education, observing, absorbing, and internalizing rules that were neither spoken nor rational but enforced through fear, intuition, and lived experience.

Even within the ordinary life of a neighborhood, the house projected a subtle menace. Casual observers could not detect the tension beneath the surface; the hum of normality continued unabated. Yet inside, the house's hidden compartments, beneath-the-floorboard vaults, and reinforced basements were extensions of the Wests' control. These spaces were both literal and symbolic, representing the power the couple wielded and the lengths to which they would go to maintain secrecy.

It was a house of layers, a structure that functioned as home and prison simultaneously. The floorboards concealed more than timber—they concealed evidence, victims, and the dark truth of Cromwell Street. Every renovation, every alteration, every repair contributed to an environment where horror and domesticity coexisted seamlessly, where silence was armor, and where secrets beneath the floorboards governed life above.

And so, life went on. Children played and studied, neighbors waved from the street, meals were prepared and eaten. But beneath the veneer of ordinariness, the house maintained its terrible rhythm. The hidden spaces were the final arbiters of control, the silent witnesses to disappearances that would only be fully understood decades later. The lessons they taught—obedience, caution, and the necessity of silence—were seared into the consciousness of those who lived there.

Cromwell Street had become a house defined by its hidden truths, its invisible victims, and its imperceptible power. The floorboards were both shield and prison, concealing horrors too terrible to name, shaping the lives of the children who survived by observation, and holding the forgotten, waiting for the day when the secrets beneath would finally be revealed.

Chapter 8

The Neighbors' Questions

C romwell Street had long been a quiet lane in Gloucester, lined with modest brick homes and tidy gardens, where neighbors were acquainted by sight and occasional small talk, but rarely by intimacy. Life here was predictable; postmen arrived with routine precision, children played on the pavements under watchful parental eyes, and neighbors nodded over fences. For decades, 25 Cromwell Street fit seamlessly into this pattern. Fred and Rosemary West were, outwardly, ordinary members of the community: Fred, the cheerful handyman, always ready to help fix a fence or mend a leaking gutter; Rosemary, the diligent housewife, impeccably polite, smiling in the right places, nodding in agreement with casual conversation. From the outside, there was nothing to suggest that this home, like all the others, held secrets that would shatter the tranquility of the neighborhood forever.

Yet subtle anomalies had begun to ripple through Cromwell Street, small enough to escape full attention but persistent enough to provoke unease in those attuned to detail. Mrs. Henshaw, who lived across the street, remembered first noticing the comings and goings of young lodgers. They arrived with hope, often timid, sometimes bright-eyed and eager, yet their departures were never announced, never discussed, and often inexplicably sudden. She found herself remarking on it once in passing to a friend: "They seem... transient, don't they? One day they're here, the next... gone." At the time, she laughed off the observation, attributing it to youth and necessity, yet a subtle unease lingered, an instinctive sense that there was more beneath the surface.

The children's laughter—once a comforting, familiar sound—also began to register differently. Some neighbors noted their silence when adults were near, the way they sometimes lingered on the doorstep as if hesitant to cross the threshold. Heather West, the eldest, and her siblings appeared well-mannered and obedient, yet observers remarked on the occasional tension in their posture, the furtive glances, the quiet demeanor that never quite matched that of carefree children on the street. These subtle cues planted seeds of curiosity, though none at the time could articulate why the household felt slightly off.

Among the more observant neighbors, questions began to form—soft, whispered, never directly addressed, yet persistent. Mr. Lloyd, who lived two doors down, occasionally caught glimpses of adults moving with quiet urgency through the living room windows, shadows that did not align with the time of day or the flow of activity. Mrs. Price, the retired schoolteacher, noted that lodgers seldom seemed to linger past a week or two; their absences were unexplained, and attempts to ask Fred or Rosemary for clarification were met with friendly but deflective smiles. The Wests had perfected the art of plausible deniability.

As the years wore on, patterns became harder to ignore, though fear and social convention constrained action. Gloucester was not a place where neighbors pried too deeply into the affairs of working-class families. There was a tacit understanding: polite inquiry was acceptable, suspicion was not. Even those who noticed discrepancies— lodgers arriving and leaving without explanation, occasional cries muffled by the walls, Rosemary's constant vigilance—hesitated to press. Questioning could provoke anger, and in a small town, confrontation carried social consequences.

Yet curiosity is persistent. In small clusters, neighbors exchanged observations quietly, in hushed tones, often under the guise of casual gossip: "Did you see that girl come in yesterday?" "She was gone by tonight." "Funny, isn't it?" They spoke cautiously, half in jest, half in genuine concern. Their questions, however, remained incomplete, circling the periphery of reality without touching the horror that lay beneath. Cromwell Street was a house that could deflect scrutiny with charm, politeness, and routine; it was a master of evasion, and the neighbors were its unwitting audience.

Fred and Rosemary, for their part, remained alert to this subtle web of observation. Fred's geniality was a shield, his jokes and offers of help a distraction. Rosemary, keenly perceptive, monitored the neighborhood for signs of suspicion. Together, they managed a delicate balance: projecting warmth and normalcy while carefully managing who saw what. A neighbor asking too many questions could be charmed into complacency, diverted with small gestures of friendliness, or simply ignored. Those who seemed overly inquisitive were met with enough social niceties to prevent confrontation, a psychological deflection as effective as any physical barrier.

There were moments, however, when tension surfaced in small but telling ways. A visiting neighbor might notice the absence of certain lodgers, the eerie silence in parts of the house, or the slight odor that sometimes drifted from the basement on humid days. Children on the street noticed whispered conversations between adults, and some neighbors began to sense that the house held stories it was not ready to tell. Mrs. Henshaw, in particular, recalled a late summer evening when she saw Heather West standing at the doorway, face pale, eyes fixed on some distant point. There was a stillness in that posture that unnerved her. She could not understand why at the time, but the memory would linger long after the street had returned to its outwardly calm appearance.

Social norms compounded the reluctance to probe further. The Wests' home was a model of domesticity: flowers in the window boxes, a freshly painted fence, curtains drawn in the evenings to maintain privacy. In a community that prized neighborliness without intrusion, outward appearances carried immense weight. And yet, questions continued to form, often unspoken, sometimes expressed in whispered conversations at church, at the local market, or over the garden fence. These murmurs, small and fragmented, created a mosaic of suspicion and intuition that, in retrospect, contained more truth than anyone at the time realized.

By the late 1980s, the convergence of repeated anomalies, inconsistent lodger departures, and the subtle behaviors of the children created a growing tension within the neighborhood. Each observation, taken alone, seemed minor. Each question, unasked or half-formed, seemed inconsequential. But together, they formed the outline of a reality that no one could yet name. The house, in its quiet mastery of concealment, remained untouchable, a fortress of normality concealing darkness. The neighbors' questions, persistent and probing, were echoes of instinct, incomplete fragments of a truth that lay buried beneath the floorboards and behind walls.

Even as they spoke in hushed tones, the neighbors unknowingly played a part in the Wests' system. By focusing on small oddities and dismissing them as quirks of domestic life, they allowed Fred and Rosemary to continue, unchallenged, the slow, deliberate accumulation of their crimes. The house remained a puzzle, one that even the most curious could not piece together. It was a stage upon which ordinary life played, masking horror beneath every creak, shadow, and half-closed curtain.

And so, Cromwell Street continued to operate with its dual realities intact. Life above the floorboards carried on—children attended school, adults went to work, neighbors exchanged pleasantries—while life beneath continued in silence, hidden, meticulously maintained. The questions that arose from neighbors were scattered and incomplete, like fragments of a larger narrative they were not yet capable of understanding. They were the first threads of awareness, delicate and tentative, that would, decades later, connect with investigation and evidence to reveal the full, unimaginable truth of the Wests' dominion over their home, their victims, and even the neighborhood itself.

In the end, the neighbors' questions were both a warning and a promise: the surface of normalcy could only hide so much, and the instincts of those who sensed danger—if followed—might one day uncover what lay beneath the polished exterior of 25 Cromwell Street. But in the moment, the questions remained unanswered, hovering on the edge of comprehension, like shadows beneath the hills, waiting for the light of discovery to illuminate the darkness.

Chapter 9

The Break in the Wall

The house at 25 Cromwell Street had always seemed ordinary to those passing by, yet inside, it had been a theater of carefully concealed horror. Each layer of plaster, every beam and floorboard, held the weight of secrets decades in the making. By the late 1980s, the first fissures in the carefully constructed façade began to appear, subtle hints that would later lead to an unimaginable revelation.

Detective Sergeant John Smith and his team approached the house with a combination of caution and grim anticipation. To the outside world, it was a tidy home: freshly painted brickwork, curtains drawn in neat folds, and children whose politeness belied the turbulence they had long endured. Yet Smith, experienced and methodical, felt the tension beneath the surface. There was an almost imperceptible distortion in the rhythm of domestic life, a pattern in the silences, a dissonance in the small gestures that, when combined, suggested the extraordinary might lie hidden.

Initial searches were meticulous. Every doorway was examined, every floorboard tapped, every corner scrutinized for anomalies. The basement, long forbidden to the children and subtly off-limits to lodgers, drew the most attention. Its air was cooler, damper, and heavier than the rest of the house. Smith noted subtle inconsistencies in the plaster and faint outlines of walls that had clearly been altered. These were not the cracks of age but deliberate modifications, signs of concealment perfected over years.

As the team began to breach the first false wall, the reality of the Wests' meticulous planning became painfully clear. Layer after layer of timber, concrete, and brick had been constructed to resist intrusion, hiding spaces within spaces. The officers found small, personal items—fragments of clothing, jewelry, and trinkets—that belonged to people who had vanished without explanation. Each item was a ghost of a life interrupted, a trace of presence now folded into the architecture itself.

Hours passed as the team carefully worked through the reinforced sections, revealing compartments that seemed impossibly concealed. The hidden spaces were designed not only to obscure but to psychologically disorient; they were tight, labyrinthine, and entirely out of the realm of ordinary domestic construction. Smith noted how Fred's expertise as a builder had been weaponized, transforming everyday materials into instruments of secrecy. The compartments were lined, reinforced, and situated so that the house itself became a silent accomplice, masking the unimaginable.

The psychological toll of the discovery weighed heavily on the officers. Each revelation was a jarring juxtaposition of normality and horror. Rooms that had appeared mundane—neatly made beds, carefully stacked books, a humming kitchen—now hid evidence of cruelty and predation. Every object recovered, every hidden space exposed, expanded the understanding of what had transpired behind the walls. The house was no longer a home; it had become a repository for the missing, a mausoleum of secrecy and terror.

For the children, the break in the wall marked a profound rupture in their lived reality. Heather and her siblings had long carried knowledge unspoken, memories that were both a curse and a survival mechanism. Now, decades later, the walls that had shaped their obedience, fear, and silence were physically breached. Their parents' authority, once absolute, was shattered by the realization that the house itself had been complicit in concealment. The team's careful excavation of hidden spaces allowed the children, for the first time, to see tangible proof of the disappearances they had sensed but never named.

Evidence collected was painstakingly documented. Investigators photographed, cataloged, and cross-referenced each item with missing-person reports. Items that might once have seemed trivial—a locket, a piece of torn fabric, a personal diary—became critical evidence, small threads in a tapestry of horror that stretched across decades. The sheer scale of concealment was staggering. Hidden walls, reinforced floors, and secret chambers revealed a systematic orchestration that had transformed the home into both trap and tomb.

As the search expanded into other areas of the house, more irregularities emerged. False panels were discovered behind kitchen cupboards, beneath staircases, and even in ceilings where ceiling boards bore faint impressions of long-concealed storage. Each compartment was both a physical and symbolic reinforcement of the control the Wests had exerted over their environment, over the victims, and over their own children. It was a house designed for invisibility, built to normalize horror through meticulous, everyday deception.

Psychologists and criminal profilers later examined the implications of these discoveries. The Wests' integration of concealment into domestic life revealed a chilling duality: the outwardly mundane home masking a methodical, predatory system. For the children, the architectural manipulations mirrored their psychological conditioning. Every hidden wall, every secret compartment, reinforced lessons in silence, vigilance, and obedience. They had been raised in a space where perception was manipulated, and reality could be folded, hidden, and obscured by those in power.

The officers' work drew out the hidden stories. Each item retrieved prompted reflection on the lives of those who had vanished. Names that had been forgotten, details once dismissed as routine absences, and fragments of lives began to reconstruct a terrifying mosaic. The house, once silent and impenetrable, was slowly revealing the scope of the Wests' control and the tragic fates of their victims.

By the end of the week-long operation, Cromwell Street had been irrevocably transformed in the eyes of the law. It was no longer a domestic residence; it was a forensic landscape, a layered structure of evidence that testified to years of deliberate manipulation, coercion, and violence. For the community, for the investigators, and for the West children, the break in the wall signified the first tangible breach of a world built on deception, fear, and silence.

As the final compartments were opened, and the last fragments of concealed evidence cataloged, a sobering realization took hold: the house had been complicit in its own horrors, a silent participant in concealment and death. Every wall, floor, and ceiling had been enlisted to protect the perpetrators, shield the victims, and maintain the illusion of ordinary life. And yet, despite decades of invisibility, the truth could not be contained any longer. The break in the wall had begun the unraveling—a fissure that would eventually expose the full depth of what had transpired at 25 Cromwell Street.

For the children, it was both liberation and trauma. Their lives, defined by fear and obedience, were now intertwined with the evidence of unspoken horrors. The walls that had dictated the rhythm of their days, the hidden spaces that had reinforced silence, were physically breached, revealing the full, harrowing reality of the household. Survival, once dependent on invisibility and compliance, now coexisted with the knowledge of exposure and justice.

The house, so long a vessel of terror and secrecy, was finally revealing its darkest truths. And as investigators worked through the layers of concealment, the shadow of Cromwell Street stretched across Gloucester, touching every family, every neighbor, and every life that had, knowingly or unknowingly, brushed against its hidden horrors.

Chapter 10

Discovery Beneath the Patio

The air in Gloucester was cool that March morning, but the stillness that surrounded 25 Cromwell Street was unnerving. What began as a quiet investigation into missing persons was about to erupt into one of the most horrifying discoveries in British criminal history. The "break in the wall" had been shocking enough, but what awaited the officers beneath the patio would shatter every illusion of normalcy that had clung to the Wests' home.

Detective Sergeant John Smith and his team had already uncovered concealed compartments within the basement—spaces too deliberate, too engineered to be innocent. Still, they had not yet found what they truly suspected. The officers had reason to believe that something far darker lay buried deeper within the property—something no one had dared imagine.

Neighbors watched from their windows as police vans and forensic units arrived quietly. The front garden, with its simple potted plants and small decorative stones, gave no hint of what was buried just below. Fred West had always been seen tending to that garden, often cheerful, even humming to himself as he mixed cement or repositioned slabs of concrete. He seemed a man proud of his handiwork, often joking with passersby about his "DIY projects." No one realized those projects had been burial rituals.

The digging began cautiously. Every movement of the spade was deliberate, the soil lifted carefully, sifted, and examined. Hours passed, then days. The first unearthed items were small—buttons, fragments of cloth, a bone too small to identify. Forensic experts were summoned. Soon after, they confirmed what every officer feared: human remains.

The site quickly transformed into a controlled excavation zone. Tarps were erected to shield the view from the growing crowd of onlookers. Reporters began to appear, whispering theories. Police cordons expanded, and Cromwell Street became the center of a grim spectacle. The discovery beneath the patio was no longer rumor—it was fact.

Fred West was called in for questioning. His demeanor was disturbingly calm. When confronted about the remains, he didn't flinch. "You'll find a few," he allegedly remarked, almost with a strange sense of relief. "I'll tell you where to look." That moment marked the unraveling of his constructed lies. The charm that had once disarmed everyone—from lodgers to neighbors—now fell away, revealing a man fully aware of the darkness he had buried.

As investigators followed his directions, they began to uncover a sequence of graves, each separated by layers of soil and cement. Beneath the concrete patio were the skeletal remains of multiple young women—each one missing for years, their fates unspoken until now. Personal items were found alongside the remains—jewelry, scraps of clothing, hair accessories—silent witnesses to the horror that had taken place within those walls.

Each body told its own story of brutality. The forensic team worked painstakingly to recover the evidence, documenting every position, every fragment, every sign of violence. It became clear that these were not impulsive acts but carefully calculated crimes, executed with precision. Fred's skill as a builder had been transformed into a means of permanent concealment, turning a home into a cemetery.

Rosemary West, too, began to feel the weight of exposure. While she maintained composure on the surface, the calm began to crack as more discoveries were made. Police noted her erratic behavior—one moment distant, the next furious. She denied involvement, portraying herself as another victim of Fred's control, yet those who knew the couple suspected complicity. Witnesses recalled her cruelty, her sudden mood changes, and her cold indifference to the lodgers who vanished.

The garden excavation expanded to include other parts of the property—the cellar, the bathroom, even the small courtyard. Every corner yielded more evidence, each revelation tightening the noose around Fred and Rosemary's carefully constructed lies. It was a painstaking process, stretching over weeks, with officers often working late into the night under floodlights.

The people of Gloucester were in disbelief. How could such horror exist in their midst, behind the neat façade of a family home? The Wests had been ordinary neighbors—friendly, unassuming, always willing to lend a tool or offer a wave. Now, that same home was being dismantled piece by piece, each shovelful of earth unearthing the truth they had hidden for nearly two decades.

When word reached the families of missing women—lodgers, hitchhikers, runaways who had disappeared without trace—the grief was overwhelming. Parents who had long clung to hope were forced to face reality. Some came to the site, standing silently across the police barriers, praying for answers, no matter how painful.

By the time the excavation concluded, police had uncovered the remains of multiple victims, all women who had vanished between the early 1970s and the 1980s. Each discovery deepened the sense of horror, yet also strengthened the resolve to ensure justice was done. Cromwell Street had become a crime scene unlike any other—a place where evil had lived undetected for years, hidden beneath layers of concrete and denial.

Fred West's demeanor shifted once again as the investigation intensified. His cooperative tone gave way to defensiveness, his stories changing with each interrogation. He claimed at times that Rosemary knew nothing, and at others that she had been the instigator. The truth, tangled in manipulation and shared guilt, was as complex as the crimes themselves.

By the end of March 1994, the world's media had descended upon Gloucester. Reporters from across the globe camped outside the cordoned area, documenting every movement of the investigation. "The House of Horrors," they called it—a name that would stick long after 25 Cromwell Street was demolished.

For the officers who worked the scene, the discovery beneath the patio was more than evidence—it was a revelation of the unimaginable capacity for cruelty that could exist behind closed doors. Each artifact, each bone, each fragment of cemented soil was a whisper from the past, telling a story of suffering that had been buried but not forgotten.

And for the people of Gloucester, it marked the end of innocence. The home they once passed without thought had become a symbol of horror, a grim reminder that monsters do not always lurk in shadows—they sometimes live next door.

Chapter 11

The Interrogations Begin

The morning Fred and Rosemary West were taken in for questioning, Gloucester seemed to hold its breath. The quiet hum of daily life—cars, footsteps, chatter—felt subdued beneath the shadow of what was unfolding. 25 Cromwell Street had already surrendered its first secrets, but the investigation had only just begun. What lay ahead would test the patience, endurance, and emotional strength of every detective who sat across from the couple.

Fred was brought in first. He appeared strangely composed, even cheerful, his familiar grin flickering across his face as though he believed he could charm his way through the storm. Dressed neatly, he joked with officers, asked for a cup of tea, and spoke with the casual tone of a man discussing home repairs rather than mass murder. Beneath that calm exterior, however, detectives sensed calculation. His demeanor wasn't ignorance—it was control, the same kind he had exercised over his victims and family for years.

Rosemary, by contrast, was cold, defensive, and visibly irritated. Her eyes darted between officers with an intensity that made even seasoned detectives uneasy. She denied everything from the start, claiming ignorance and painting herself as a victim of Fred's "dark side." Yet the tension between them was palpable. They avoided eye contact. The bond that had once united them in cruelty was beginning to fracture under the pressure of truth.

Detective Superintendent John Bennett led the interrogation process. He understood that men like Fred West did not respond to force or intimidation—they responded to attention, to being heard. The officers let Fred talk, giving him room to weave his stories. At first, his account was filled with half-truths and misdirection. He admitted to "helping" women who had fallen on hard times, offering them lodging and work. When pressed about the remains beneath the patio, he deflected. "Some of them wanted to stay," he said. "Some didn't."

Gradually, inconsistencies began to surface. Dates didn't align. Names that Fred mentioned were later linked to missing persons reports. As hours turned into days, his confidence began to erode. The charm faltered. The smirk faded. When officers mentioned the names of his own children—particularly those who had lived in the house during the disappearances—Fred's mask slipped. He hesitated, his words stumbling as he tried to separate the lies from the fragments of truth.

The investigators employed patience and subtlety. They knew that Fred's ego was both his defense and his weakness. By allowing him to feel in control, they lured him deeper into contradiction. Each interview was carefully documented, every phrase analyzed. At times, he spoke as though describing another person's actions, distancing himself from responsibility. "Things got out of hand," he murmured once, his gaze fixed on the floor. "Rose didn't like some of them… she could be cruel."

Meanwhile, Rosemary's interrogations followed a different rhythm. She refused to answer most questions, insisting that she knew nothing. Her denial was absolute, her anger sharp. When confronted with Fred's partial admissions, she erupted into outrage. "He's lying to save himself!" she shouted. "I had nothing to do with any of it!" Yet even in her fury, detectives noticed subtle cracks—moments when her expression changed, when a particular name or location made her flinch ever so slightly.

Psychologists were brought in to observe the pair. Their assessment was chilling: Fred displayed traits of narcissistic and antisocial personality disorders, while Rosemary exhibited extreme emotional detachment, control, and volatility. Together, they had formed a partnership of domination and manipulation, each feeding the other's worst impulses. Their relationship was not merely romantic—it was symbiotic and destructive.

As the questioning intensified, Fred began to talk more freely, almost as if unburdening himself. He offered details that were not yet public knowledge—descriptions of rooms, methods of restraint, and the precise placement of graves. Each revelation sent waves of disbelief through the team. It was not just the brutality of his acts that horrified them, but the casual, almost routine manner in which he described them.

"I built the place to last," he once said, with eerie pride. "No one was ever supposed to find them."

Despite his growing openness, Fred remained selective. He confessed to certain acts but remained vague about others, especially those implicating Rosemary. When investigators sensed he was shielding her, they pressed harder. Eventually, his tone changed. He began to speak of "we," of "us," of shared actions that blurred the line between his guilt and hers.

Rosemary, on the other hand, grew increasingly agitated as Fred talked. When informed of his statements, she denied them vehemently, claiming he was fabricating stories to destroy her. But her reactions grew erratic. Officers noted her emotional instability—tears one moment, icy composure the next. The psychological tug-of-war between them became a battle of blame, each trying to shift responsibility onto the other as the evidence mounted.

In one particularly tense session, Fred was shown photographs of the excavation—the skeletal remains, the small personal items unearthed from beneath the concrete. He stared at them in silence, his expression blank. Then, after a long pause, he whispered, "They didn't deserve that. None of them did." It was the closest he ever came to remorse.

Behind the scenes, forensic experts were meticulously piecing together the evidence. Each discovery from Cromwell Street was matched to missing persons files, cross-referenced with testimonies, and examined for DNA traces. The picture that emerged was horrifyingly clear: this was a calculated pattern of abduction, torture, and murder spanning decades.

As days turned into weeks, Fred's resolve began to crumble. He spoke more freely, revealing new burial sites beyond Cromwell Street—fields, gardens, and old construction sites. Each revelation sent search teams scrambling across Gloucestershire, uncovering further evidence of the Wests' long campaign of cruelty.

Rosemary was soon confronted with Fred's confessions. She sat motionless as officers read his statements aloud, her face a mask of contained fury. "He's trying to ruin me," she said coldly. "If he's guilty, let him rot. But don't you dare put me with him." Her tone carried both contempt and fear—fear that the façade she had carefully maintained was crumbling beyond repair.

Eventually, the interrogations became less about extracting confessions and more about documenting the full extent of the crimes. Both Fred and Rosemary were charged with multiple counts of murder. For detectives who had lived and breathed the case, it was both a victory and a burden. The truth had finally begun to emerge, but it came at a cost—the haunting knowledge of what had taken place in that ordinary-looking home.

When Fred was escorted from the interrogation room for the last time, he looked strangely calm, even relieved. "It's all over now," he said softly. "No more lies." But for those who had heard his words, the echoes of his confessions would never fade.

And for Rosemary, who sat alone in her cell, the walls of denial were closing in. The partnership that had once defined her existence was gone, replaced by isolation and fear. The interrogations had done what decades of secrecy could not—they had exposed the truth.

The truth of what they had done.

And the truth of who they really were.

Chapter 12

The Confessions of Fred West

In the cold, gray confines of the Gloucester Police Station, the man who had once walked through life with a smile and a joke now sat under a harsh strip of light. Fred West's face, weathered and uneven, carried the expression of a man uncertain of what he had lost or what he had finally been cornered into revealing. The hum of the fluorescent lamp above him was constant, a soundless metronome ticking off the seconds of a life closing in.

Detective Chief Inspector John Bennett sat across from him, pen in hand, his gaze steady but calm. Between them sat a cup of untouched tea, now cold, and a tape recorder waiting for truth. For weeks, the walls of Cromwell Street had spoken without words — evidence unearthed from the earth, belongings found beneath floors and patios — and now it was Fred's turn to speak. What began as denial would soon unravel into something darker: a confession that would change British criminal history forever.

At first, Fred's voice was calm, conversational, even friendly. He spoke as if telling stories from memory — detached, almost boastful in tone. "I helped a few girls out," he began, shrugging lightly. "They had nowhere to go. Some were runaways. You know how it is, officer. I gave them food, a place to sleep. Maybe too much trust. Maybe too much kindness."

Detective Bennett said nothing. He knew better than to interrupt a man trying to make himself sound harmless. He simply watched, waiting for the cracks to form. They always did.

Fred shifted in his chair, eyes darting to the corners of the room as though searching for an escape that no longer existed. "Some of them left. Some... didn't," he added finally, his tone dropping. "That's what you're here about, isn't it? The ones that didn't."

Silence stretched, thick and suffocating. The tape whirred softly. Fred's fingers trembled slightly as he reached for the cigarette he wasn't allowed to smoke. His hands found only the table.

It was not one confession, but a slow unfurling of many. Fred's story began in fragments — half-truths, diversions, occasional blame shifted to Rosemary. He was a man skilled in manipulation, and even in custody, he sought control of the narrative. "You see," he said, leaning forward, "Rose... she had a temper. She could be cruel. I tried to stop her sometimes. But once you've started something, you can't just stop it, can you?"

The detectives exchanged glances but said nothing. They knew his method: minimize his role, amplify hers. Yet with each question, each detail he offered, he drew himself deeper into the truth. As the hours passed, the confidence wavered. His sentences began to fracture, his memories conflicting, his justifications turning hollow.

On the third day of interrogation, when the photographs were placed before him — bones found under the patio, fragments of personal items recovered from the garden — Fred's demeanor changed. His eyes softened, almost mournful. The façade cracked.

"That one," he whispered, pointing to a small silver ring. "That was Anne Marie's friend. She was only supposed to stay a few nights."

He paused, his breath catching. "I told Rose we couldn't keep her. She didn't listen. Things got out of hand."

Detective Bennett's pen stilled. "Out of hand?" he repeated softly.

Fred nodded, eyes downcast. "We didn't mean for it to happen. But once she was gone... well, you can't leave things lying about, can you? You've got to clean up. That's what I did. I cleaned up."

He said it so plainly, as though describing a chore. But behind the words was the revelation of systematic horror. Each sentence opened another door, and behind each door was another grave.

Over the following sessions, the confessions deepened. Fred began to recall names, years, and rooms in chilling detail. He remembered the soil he had mixed, the layers of concrete poured to hide what could not be spoken aloud. At times, his voice trembled not from guilt, but from fatigue — the exhaustion of holding onto a secret that had finally grown too heavy.

Rosemary, meanwhile, sat in another room, silent and motionless. Her denial was absolute, her anger ice-cold. "He's lying," she told detectives repeatedly. "He always lies." But there was something in her eyes — a flicker of recognition when certain names were mentioned — that betrayed her.

As Fred spoke, her world began to collapse. The empire of control they had built together was dissolving under the weight of his words.

Fred's confessions were not linear. They came in loops, in contradictions, in sudden bursts of clarity followed by stretches of silence. One moment he was calm; the next, tearful. He spoke of his childhood, of abuse, of loneliness, of the need to dominate. He seemed to shift between identities — the victim, the worker, the father, the killer — as if searching for one that could absolve him.

"I didn't want to hurt them," he said once, voice cracking. "But something happens inside me. I can't explain it. It's like... it's like a storm. Once it starts, I can't stop it."

When Bennett asked him why he buried the bodies beneath his own home, Fred looked up and smiled faintly. "Because they'd always be near," he said. "I knew where they were. Safe, you could say."

It was in that moment that even the seasoned detectives felt an unspoken chill. Fred's sense of "safety" was rooted in control — a need to possess every trace of the lives he had destroyed. Beneath the ordinary words lay the psychology of a man who sought permanence in domination.

Beyond the interview room, the impact of Fred's confessions spread like a shockwave. The officers who dug at Cromwell Street carried the memory of every discovery — bones wrapped in plastic, personal items clutched as though in final defense. Families of the missing women sat in waiting rooms, clutching photographs that now felt like relics of another world.

For Fred's children, each revelation tore another thread from their already fragile understanding of family. They listened to reports on the radio, saw the headlines, and struggled to reconcile the father who had smiled at breakfast with the monster described in court briefings. The man who had once built sandcastles with them at the beach had also built tombs beneath their home.

Rosemary remained unyielding. She refused to acknowledge the depth of Fred's admissions, calling them "fantasies" or "twisted tales." Yet the detectives knew her silence was strategic — an armor of denial. Fred, meanwhile, began to seek sympathy in confession, positioning himself as misunderstood. "I didn't force anyone," he said in one of his later interviews. "They stayed because they wanted to. They trusted me."

Detective Bennett, now visibly weary, leaned forward. "Fred," he said quietly, "trust doesn't end with bones under concrete."

For the first time, Fred said nothing.

As days turned into weeks, the cumulative pressure of evidence — both physical and psychological — began to crush what was left of Fred's self-deception. Late one evening, he requested another interview. "I want to get it all out," he told the guards. "No more bits and pieces. All of it."

When the recorder clicked on, he began in a flat, subdued tone. "There were twelve," he said. "Maybe more.

I lost count after a while. You dig under that house — you'll find them all."

He named them slowly, sometimes pausing as if reaching into the fog of memory. Each name was a door opening to the unthinkable. His voice faltered when he mentioned his own daughter, Heather. "That one hurt the most," he said quietly. "But she knew too much. She was going to talk. I couldn't let her."

The room fell silent. Even the hum of the light seemed to fade.

After that night, Fred's tone changed. The bravado was gone. What remained was a strange calm, as though unburdened by the truth. "I've said my piece," he told Bennett the following morning. "It's all out now. The rest's up to you."

Detectives left the room with the heavy knowledge that they had heard everything they needed — and far more than they wished to.

Fred's confessions became the backbone of the prosecution case, yet they also revealed a psyche so fractured that truth and self-delusion intertwined. His words carried both horror and emptiness. Some officers later described the interviews as "listening to evil narrate itself," not through rage or madness, but through calm recollection.

As the investigation reached its height, Fred's mental state began to deteriorate. He became withdrawn, anxious, paranoid that Rosemary would betray him. "She'll make it all my fault," he muttered repeatedly. "But she was there. She did it too."

In those final weeks before his trial, Fred's confessions stopped altogether. He avoided eye contact, refused food, and spoke only in fragments. On January 1, 1995, he was found dead in his prison cell — a suicide note beside him that read, simply:

"Rose, it's you and me forever. No one else."

Fred West's confessions had begun as lies, twisted through self-defense and manipulation, but by the end, they had become something far more haunting — the written record of a life spent destroying others to fill the emptiness within himself. His words, preserved on tape and paper, remain among the most chilling documents in British criminal history.

And yet, for all his admissions, there were still questions unanswered — gaps in the timeline, missing names, unspoken truths that would never be recovered. The silence that followed his death was almost as disturbing as the confessions themselves.

For those who had listened — the detectives, the families, the surviving children — that silence was not peace. It was an echo.

A reminder that even when a monster finally speaks, the truth can never fully heal what has been buried.

Chapter 13

The Trial of Rosemary West

The courtroom in Winchester Crown Court stood cold and unforgiving, its walls echoing with the weight of history and the scent of dread. It was 1995, and for months, the world had watched with bated breath as one of Britain's darkest sagas approached its reckoning. Fred West was gone—he had taken his secrets to the grave in a lonely cell—but his wife, Rosemary West, remained. The trial that now bore her name would attempt the impossible: to untangle the truth from decades of deceit, terror, and silence.

When Rosemary entered the courtroom for the first time, she appeared composed, her expression calm in a way that disturbed many. Her dark hair framed a face that betrayed nothing—no remorse, no fear, not even surprise.

To those who had followed the horrors of 25 Cromwell Street, she was no longer merely a suspect; she was the living embodiment of unanswered questions. Who was she when the doors were closed? A victim of Fred's manipulation—or his willing accomplice?

The prosecution sought to answer that question with evidence that painted a portrait of cold collaboration. They spoke of the girls who had vanished, of the bodies found beneath floorboards and patios, and of the children who had lived through unspeakable nightmares. Each name read aloud carried a weight that hung in the air—Charmaine, Heather, Shirley, and the rest—echoing like a funeral bell.

Rosemary's defense argued that she had been under Fred's control, subjected to years of abuse and coercion, molded by fear into silence. Yet the testimony from those who had survived contradicted that claim. Her surviving children spoke in trembling voices of their mother's cruelty, her sudden fits of rage, her participation in punishments that went far beyond discipline. To them, Fred may have been the architect of terror, but Rosemary had been its keeper.

Day after day, the courtroom heard stories that tested the endurance of everyone present. Pathologists described the grim discoveries at Cromwell Street in precise, clinical tones. Investigators spoke of the unearthed bones and the meticulous concealment of each victim. It was not only evidence being presented—it was an autopsy of evil itself.

Witnesses took the stand, some of them visibly shaking as they recalled their encounters with the Wests. Neighbors spoke of laughter from behind the walls, the sudden disappearances of young lodgers, and the uneasy feeling that something had always been wrong. Police officers described the smell of decay, the dread of excavation, the sound of shovels breaking through lies that had been buried for decades.

Through it all, Rosemary sat impassively, occasionally scribbling notes, occasionally glancing toward the jury with an unreadable calm. The press tried to decipher her— was she haunted or hollow? A woman trapped by her husband's madness or a monster in her own right?

When the tapes of Fred's interviews were played, the courtroom fell silent. His voice, crude and casual, recounted unspeakable acts as if they were chores on an ordinary day. He spoke of "fun and games," of "keeping things quiet," of "burying them properly." He never condemned Rosemary. In his warped way, he shielded her, perhaps still loyal to the woman who had shared his twisted world. But even in his protection, the cracks were visible. His words hinted at her involvement—her presence, her anger, her control.

By the time closing arguments began, the evidence had drawn a chilling picture. Rosemary West was charged with ten counts of murder—each one a story of betrayal, cruelty, and unimaginable suffering. The prosecution's voice was steady as they described her as "an active participant in a series of murders that shocked the conscience of the nation."

Her defense, desperate and thin, pleaded for the jury to see her as a broken woman molded by abuse, manipulated into compliance. But even they seemed to sense the futility of their case. The weight of what had been uncovered at Cromwell Street could not be lightened by excuses.

The jury retired for deliberation. Outside, the press swarmed like vultures. Inside, the families of victims sat in hushed anticipation. Hours stretched into days before the verdict was delivered. When the foreman stood, the courtroom froze.

"Guilty," he said. Once. Then again. Then again. Ten times in total.

Rosemary West showed no visible emotion. No tears, no gasp, no word. She stood as if made of stone, her face pale but steady, as the judge pronounced a life sentence without the possibility of parole.

In that moment, the silence that followed was deafening. Some of the families wept quietly; others simply stared at her, trying to reconcile the image of the woman before them with the atrocities she had helped conceal. The trial had ended, but the horror of what it revealed would echo far beyond that courtroom.

When Rosemary was led away, the finality of her steps seemed to close a chapter of British history that many wished had never been written. Yet even then, the questions lingered. How much had she truly known? How deeply had she participated? And what had driven two people to turn an ordinary house into a graveyard of the innocent?

The verdict could bring justice, but not peace. For those who had lost their loved ones, the wounds would remain open. Cromwell Street would later be demolished, the earth beneath it cleansed, but the memory of what it had contained—what it had hidden—could never be erased.

In the end, the trial of Rosemary West was not only the story of one woman's guilt; it was the confrontation of a nation with its own capacity for darkness. The courtroom had become a mirror reflecting the unthinkable—a place where evil had once lived behind a simple door with the number 25.

And though the door was gone, and the house destroyed, its shadows would remain—etched into the minds of those who had seen, heard, and never forgotten.

Chapter 14

The Aftermath and the House That Died

The house at 25 Cromwell Street stood for years after the arrests, fenced off and silent. It loomed like a wound in the center of Gloucester — not just a building, but a reminder of everything that had gone wrong behind those ordinary brick walls. Reporters swarmed around it, cameras flashing, curious onlookers gathering at the barriers to glimpse the infamous address where horror had worn a human face. The curtains were gone, the garden overgrown, the windows boarded — yet the silence it carried was heavier than any noise.

When the police tape was finally removed, and the court cases began to wind toward their grim conclusions, the council faced a question no one wanted to answer out loud: What do you do with a house like that? Some wanted it preserved as evidence, others wanted it erased completely. Families of the victims could not bear the thought of its existence — of people driving by, pointing, turning cruelty into spectacle. Yet the investigators still needed time. Beneath its crumbling foundations, there were still stories to uncover, fragments to collect, and souls to account for.

Inside the police archives, the evidence room had become a mausoleum of its own. Boxes labeled 25 Cromwell Streetfilled shelves from floor to ceiling: clothing fibers, jewelry, bones, soil samples, notebooks, broken tools. The ordinary objects of daily life — a comb, a shoe, a torn photograph — sat sealed in clear plastic bags, stripped of context but loaded with meaning. Forensic specialists worked tirelessly to match DNA samples to missing persons, reconstructing timelines from chaos. In every photograph, the house was present like a character itself: cruel, mute, and patient.

Gloucester had always been a quiet city, proud of its heritage and its community. But now, whispers traveled through its streets like wind through a graveyard. Parents clutched their children's hands tighter. Shopkeepers lowered their voices when discussing the case. Neighbors who once exchanged morning greetings now looked at each other differently, as if questioning how such atrocities could have lived among them unnoticed.

Memorials began to appear — small, delicate offerings left by strangers. Bouquets of wildflowers were laid on the pavement outside Cromwell Street, their petals bright against the grey stone. Handwritten notes spoke of grief and guilt, of regret for not seeing sooner what had been hidden in plain sight. "For all who were lost," one read. Another simply said, "We remember you."

The press, relentless and hungry, turned the tragedy into front-page obsession. Reporters camped outside the courthouse, dissecting every statement, every photograph, every whisper from inside the courtroom. Yet beneath the spectacle, there was genuine public mourning — a reckoning with the realization that monsters had walked unnoticed through familiar streets.

As Fred's fate was sealed by his own hand in a prison cell, attention turned to Rosemary West. Without Fred, she became the sole bearer of the horrors they had created together. Her trial began in 1995 at Winchester Crown Court, one of the most heavily covered trials in British legal history.

Each day, she arrived flanked by guards, her face expressionless, her eyes hidden behind glasses that reflected flashes of camera light. Inside the courtroom, families of the victims sat in tense silence. Some refused to look at her; others stared, searching for signs of remorse that never came. The prosecution presented weeks of evidence — a catalogue of brutality that stripped away any illusion of innocence. Witness after witness described the years of torment, the disappearances, the children raised in fear. The air in the courtroom often felt heavy, suffocating under the weight of the details.

When the verdict was read, there was no gasping, no shouting. Only silence — deep, final, and heavy. Rosemary West was found guilty on ten counts of murder and sentenced to life imprisonment, with a recommendation that she never be released. For the families, it was justice, but not closure. Closure implies something finished — and this pain was anything but.

After the trial, all eyes returned once again to the house. The Gloucester City Council, after long deliberation, decided that 25 Cromwell Street could not remain standing. It was no longer a home; it was a scar, a reminder too unbearable to keep. In early 1996, demolition crews arrived. The street was cordoned off, and police officers stood guard as bulldozers idled nearby. Reporters gathered beyond the barricades, their cameras ready to capture history being buried.

Before the machines moved, a small ceremony took place — quiet, unannounced, attended only by officials and a few family members. A chaplain read a brief prayer. The words were simple: "May the earth reclaim what it has seen, and may peace return to this place."

The first strike of the wrecking ball echoed through the neighborhood like a heartbeat stopping. Bricks crumbled, glass shattered, and decades of darkness fell to dust. The rooms that had once imprisoned screams were reduced to rubble, their secrets exposed to daylight at last. The basement — the most dreadful place of all — was filled with concrete, layer by layer, until there was no trace of the chambers that had stolen so many lives.

Neighbors watched in silence. Some wept. Others turned away. It wasn't triumph they felt, but exhaustion — as if an invisible weight had been lifted, leaving only sorrow behind. When the dust settled, all that remained was an empty lot surrounded by fencing. Later, it would be turned into a pedestrian walkway, open and unmarked. No plaque, no sign, no memorial. Just ordinary pavement, where footsteps would pass without knowing what lay beneath.

The surviving children of Fred and Rosemary West faced lives shadowed by their parents' crimes. Many of them were taken into care, given new identities, and relocated. Some would later speak publicly, describing years of confusion and trauma, trying to understand how love and terror could coexist within the same walls. For them, healing was not a destination but an ongoing battle — one fought in silence, therapy rooms, and sleepless nights.

Investigators, too, carried the burden. Many of the officers involved in the case struggled for years afterward. Some retired early; others found themselves haunted by memories of what they had uncovered. "You can't unsee it," one officer said years later. "You go home, and it's there. Every creak of your house reminds you of that basement."

The people of Gloucester rebuilt slowly. The press eventually moved on, the tourists stopped coming, and life resumed its rhythm. But 25 Cromwell Street had changed the city forever. It had forced a collective reckoning — not only about the evil of two individuals but about the blindness of society itself, how kindness, politeness, and privacy could allow horrors to thrive unnoticed.

In the years following the case, criminologists and psychologists dissected the minds of Fred and Rosemary West, searching for the roots of their depravity. Were they born monsters, or made by the violence of their pasts? Fred's childhood had been steeped in abuse and incest, shaping his understanding of dominance and pain. Rosemary's upbringing, too, was marked by trauma and control. But together, they created something that transcended pathology — a shared delusion of power, a partnership that thrived on secrecy and submission.

Experts described them as a "mutually reinforcing dyad" — two damaged souls whose union became catastrophic. Each satisfied the other's darkest desires, and each normalized the unspeakable for the other. Their crimes were not acts of passion, but patterns of control. And perhaps most chillingly, they disguised it all behind smiles, laughter, and domestic normality.

For psychologists studying criminal behavior, the Wests became a textbook case — not of madness, but of manipulation, the terrifying potential of ordinary people when empathy is replaced by domination.

The Cultural Echo

Years later, books, documentaries, and dramatizations would revisit the story, each trying to make sense of what had happened. But no retelling ever truly captured the dread that those who lived near Cromwell Street felt. Some residents moved away permanently, unable to live with the memories. Others stayed, determined not to let evil define their home.

One of the builders who helped demolish the house later said in an interview, "It felt like we were burying something unholy. But we were also setting people free."

And in a sense, he was right. The destruction of 25 Cromwell Street was not just the end of a structure, but the symbolic closure of an era of silence — the kind of silence that allows cruelty to grow in the dark. By erasing the house, the city reclaimed itself.

Ghosts That Never Leave

Even now, decades later, the story of Fred and Rosemary West lingers like a cold shadow over British criminal history. It remains a case that unsettles not because of its violence alone, but because of its intimacy

— the way horror had been woven into the fabric of domestic life.

Every few years, journalists still revisit the site. They find nothing — no trace, no mark, no scent of what once was. The air feels ordinary. But locals swear that on quiet mornings, when fog rolls through Gloucester, you can still feel something — a heaviness, a stillness, as if the ground itself remembers.

For the families of the victims, remembrance takes many forms: photographs on mantelpieces, anniversaries spent in private reflection, flowers left anonymously at memorials far from Cromwell Street. They live with the unanswerable questions — Why? How could it happen? — knowing that some mysteries will remain buried forever.

The House That Died, the Lives That Endured

When the last stone of Cromwell Street was cleared, and grass began to grow where once there was concrete and rot, a strange peace settled over the place. It was not forgiveness — that would never come — but a kind of surrender to time. The horrors had been unearthed, the perpetrators punished, and the ghosts given acknowledgment. What remained was memory, fragile and enduring.

In the years since, 25 Cromwell Street has become more than a location; it has become a symbol — of vigilance, of awareness, and of the darkness that can live behind ordinary doors. It is a reminder that evil often wears the most familiar face, and that silence is the soil in which it grows.

And so, the house that once stood as a monument to cruelty became something else entirely: a lesson carved into history, a warning whispered through generations.

Because though the house died, the stories it buried — and the lives it stole — would never be forgotten.

Chapter 15

Echoes That Remain

In the years that followed the demolition of 25 Cromwell Street, time did what it always does — it moved forward. Streets were repaved, new shops opened, and laughter returned to the sidewalks of Gloucester. Yet, beneath the surface of that slow return to normalcy, something invisible lingered. The ground had been disturbed by more than machinery; it had been unsettled by memory itself. Though the bricks were gone and the concrete sealed, echoes of the house remained — not in walls or shadows, but in the people who had lived, loved, lost, and survived within its orbit.

The Wests were gone. The trials were over. The headlines had faded from daily conversation. But every once in a while, the past resurfaced — in a documentary broadcast late at night, in a book found on a library shelf, or in the cautious conversation between strangers who realized they shared a connection to that dreadful street.

The house may have died, but the story never did. It lived on in whispers, in nightmares, and in the fragile spaces between memory and forgetting.

For those who had survived the Wests — their children, relatives, investigators, and neighbors — life became a long negotiation with the ghosts of what they had seen. Each person carried a fragment of the story, and each fragment carried its own weight.

Some of Fred and Rosemary's surviving children grew up in new towns under new names. Their childhoods had been a blur of rules and silence, of promises never kept and threats never forgotten. Even as adults, they struggled to separate their own identities from the infamy attached to their bloodline. One of them would later write, "You don't just escape a house like that. You carry it inside you, like a smell that never leaves."

For the children who lived through it, the hardest part was not remembering — it was trying not to. Every ordinary thing became a reminder: the sound of footsteps on stairs, the creak of a basement door, the scent of plaster or damp soil. Therapy helped, sometimes. Other times, it only stirred the pain that lay buried beneath years of forced forgetting. But they kept trying, because survival demanded it.

For the detectives who had unearthed the crimes, the memories clung to them like dust from that basement. They had entered 25 Cromwell Street as officers and left as witnesses to something far beyond criminal behavior — something that touched on the darkest edges of human capability. Some retired early, their health deteriorating under the strain of what they had uncovered. Others stayed on the force, trying to turn the horror into purpose, reminding new recruits of what vigilance meant, of what happens when small warnings go unheard.

One detective, years after his retirement, returned to the empty site. He stood there in the drizzle, hands deep in his coat pockets, watching pedestrians pass without a glance. The street was ordinary now — a walkway, some new paving stones, a lamppost humming quietly. No one knew what had once stood there. But he knew. He said later, "It wasn't the house I saw. It was the silence. The silence that let it happen."

The families of the victims never found peace, though some found endurance. They attended memorials in private, placed flowers anonymously, and carried their grief quietly. For many, the most painful truth was not only what had been done, but how long it had gone unnoticed. Years of missing person reports, ignored leads, unasked questions — all of it lingered like a cold wind in the mind. The guilt of society, the failure of neighbors, the blindness of institutions — it all formed part of the echo.

And yet, in that echo, something else began to form: a determination that it would never happen again.

Writers, psychologists, and criminologists studied the Wests for decades afterward, trying to understand the anatomy of their cruelty. They examined upbringing, mental illness, control dynamics, and sexual pathology. They traced the roots of their violence to childhood traumas and environments steeped in dominance and secrecy. But no theory ever seemed enough. Evil, they found, resists tidy explanation. It is not an event, but a slow growth — nurtured in silence, watered by neglect, and hidden behind the walls of normality.

Rosemary West remained behind bars, aging within the quiet walls of prison. She rarely spoke publicly, and when she did, her tone remained detached, her words empty of remorse. Fred's suicide had left her the only living witness to their shared crimes, yet she continued to deny her role, shifting blame, rewriting memories. To the world outside, she became a figure of morbid fascination — not merely because of what she had done, but because of how ordinary she appeared while doing it.

The British public, though long desensitized to crime stories, never truly forgot this one. There was something about the domesticity of it — the cheerful family façade, the children playing in the garden, the rented rooms — that broke through the nation's defenses. It shattered the illusion that monsters live elsewhere, far away. The Wests had not lurked in the shadows of alleys or forests; they had lived next door. They had laughed, cooked dinner, and waved at the mailman. And that realization was perhaps the most chilling of all.

For Gloucester itself, healing was a slow, almost invisible process. The lot where the house once stood became a pathway used by schoolchildren, commuters, and tourists who had no idea what ground they were walking on. Sometimes, a passerby would pause, noticing the odd quietness of that section of the street. The air seemed heavier there, the light dimmer. But most just kept walking. Perhaps that was as it should be — perhaps the earth had earned its silence.

Yet every so often, on anniversaries or in forgotten newspaper clippings, the story would reappear. Photographs of Fred and Rosemary, grainy and faded, would resurface. Commentators would discuss what the case had taught law enforcement, or how it had changed the way Britain handled missing person investigations. But behind every analytical essay and legal reform was something far simpler — grief. The grief of the families. The grief of a city that had unknowingly sheltered horror. The grief of a nation forced to see how fragile safety truly was.

The echoes of Cromwell Street reached far beyond Gloucester. They touched social services, police departments, and communities across the country. Procedures were rewritten, communication between agencies strengthened, early-warning systems put in place.

Out of tragedy, reforms were born — imperfect but necessary. That, perhaps, was the quiet redemption in the story: that some good, however small, could grow from the ruin.

But even with progress, the emotional residue of the case never faded completely. Those who studied it, wrote about it, or remembered it often described feeling haunted — not by ghosts, but by questions. How could such darkness go unseen for so long? How many warning signs had been ignored out of politeness, fear, or disbelief? And could it happen again, hidden behind another neat row of brick houses, another smiling family photo?

Somewhere in the British countryside, on a cold winter evening, a former journalist once wrote, "The story of the Wests is not about monsters. It's about people. About what happens when empathy dies, when curiosity stops, when we stop listening to the quiet cries next door."

He was right. The story was not confined to the past. It was a mirror held up to society — showing what happens when cruelty disguises itself as normality, when abuse hides behind respectability, when we choose not to see.

And yet, there were survivors — proof that even in the bleakest places, life finds ways to endure. Some of the Wests' children built families of their own. They spoke cautiously about their parents, but also about hope. "We are not them," one of them said in an interview many years later. "We are what came after."

That was the true echo — not just of pain, but of survival. For every life stolen, there were those who refused to let the story end in silence. They spoke out, educated others, and turned their trauma into warning.

Time, as always, kept moving. The rain washed away the dust, and the grass grew green over the spot where 25 Cromwell Street had once stood. Children now ran across it without fear, their laughter echoing down the street. And perhaps that was the final act of healing — that innocence could return to the very ground where it had once been destroyed.

At night, when the city quieted and the streetlights flickered, the air around that space still felt different — not haunted, but solemn, as if it remembered. The past can be buried, but it does not disappear. It becomes part of the earth, part of the story that shapes us all.

The echoes of Cromwell Street will always remain — not as screams or shadows, but as reminders. Reminders of how easily evil can hide behind ordinary walls, and how crucial it is to see, to listen, to care.

Because somewhere, in every town, there is a house that looks perfectly normal. And sometimes, that is exactly where the darkest stories begin.

Conclusion

The story of Fred and Rosemary West is one that continues to haunt not only the quiet city of Gloucester but the collective memory of an entire nation. What began as whispers in a working-class neighborhood became one of the darkest revelations in British criminal history. Yet beyond the horror lies a chilling truth about human nature — how ordinary faces can conceal extraordinary evil. The Wests' crimes did not exist in isolation; they thrived within silence, fear, and societal blind spots that allowed their cruelty to go unnoticed for far too long.

But amidst that darkness, there emerged courage — from detectives who refused to abandon missing persons' cases, from journalists who pressed for answers, and from the surviving victims and families who demanded truth even when it shattered their world. The investigation at 25 Cromwell Street was not just about uncovering bodies; it was about reclaiming stolen voices. Each life found beneath that soil was more than evidence — it was a person whose existence deserved recognition, dignity, and remembrance.

The demolition of the house symbolized an effort to erase a landmark of evil, yet it could never fully remove the scars left behind. The legacy of Fred and Rosemary West is not a tale of fascination, but of caution — a reminder that evil can wear a familiar smile and that vigilance is the price of safety. The story endures not to glorify horror, but to honor those who were silenced and to remind the world of the importance of listening when something feels wrong, even in the most ordinary of places.

Afterword

Time has a way of softening the edges of memory, but in the case of Cromwell Street, it has not dulled the unease. Today, Gloucester has rebuilt itself — new homes, new families, and new beginnings. Yet when people pass the site where number 25 once stood, they feel it: a hush, a kind of reverence mixed with sorrow. The house may be gone, but its ghost lingers in the collective conscience.

In the years since the Wests' crimes came to light, their case has become a reference point in discussions about social neglect, domestic abuse, and psychological manipulation. It has forced institutions to rethink how they respond to signs of danger — especially when those signs come from within a family home. It has also shown the resilience of those left behind — the surviving children, the relatives of victims, and the community that had to face its own complicity in years of silence.

True evil, as this story proves, is not supernatural. It hides in plain sight — in laughter over dinner, in small acts of charm, in the illusion of normality. Remembering this case is not about retelling horror for its own sake, but about ensuring that the world recognizes the warning signs it once ignored.

www.ingramcontent.com/pod-product-compliance
Ingram Content Group UK Ltd.
Pitfield, Milton Keynes, MK11 3LW, UK
UKHW020746041225
9367UKWH00031B/624